# Geographic Diversification and Export Innovation

## Zahra Nasiri

## Dr. Sahar Ahmadian
Faculty Member of Islamic Azad University, Buinzahra Branch

Title: Geographic Diversification and Export
Innovation
Authors: Zahra Nasiri , Dr. Sahar Ahmadian (Faculty
Member of Islamic Azad University, Buinzahra Branch)
Editor: Mohsen Rahmandoust
Publisher: American Academic Research, USA
ISBN: 9781947464346

# Table of Content

3

# Introduction

Innovation in export is considered a competitive advantage that ultimately leads to an increase in export performance. There are many studies in the field of export, but there are very few studies that focus on geographical borders. Geographical diversity can greatly affect the intensity of the impact of innovation on export performance. The diversity of geographical borders is a good opportunity for exporters to learn, on the other hand, geographic diversity increases costs and also causes the complexity of exports. Geographical diversity causes differences in sociocultural, technological, economic, political-legal, and ecological factors. Factors such as cultural standards, customer preferences, legal systems, international transportation costs, tariffs, customs procedures, preparation of documents, etc., all of which can greatly affect export cost. In fact, an important challenge for a company's international marketing is the need to understand different environments in different countries. In this book, we are going to talk about the issue of geographical boundaries and their impact on export innovation. We focouse on sociocultural factors.

# Chapter 1. Sociocultural Factors

In order to analyze the international environment, 5 major environments should be analyzed. These factors include socio-cultural, technological, economic, ecological, and political-legal factors. Each of these factors are different in various geographical boundaries. Table No. 1 shows these factors and their subfactors. In the following, each of the factors and its impact on export innovation will be discussed.

| Sociocultural | Technological | Economic | Ecological | Political-Legal |
|---|---|---|---|---|
| Customs, norms, values | Regulations on technology transfer | Economic development | Non-governmental groups | Form of government |
| Language | Energy availability/cost | Per capita income | Passion for environ-mental causes | Political ideology |
| Demographics | Natural resource availability | Climate | Infrastructure to handle recycling | Tax laws |
| Life expectancies | Transportation network | GDP trends | | Stability of government |
| Social institutions | Skill level of workforce | Monetary and fiscal policies | | Government atti-tude toward foreign companies |
| Status symbols | Patent-trademark protection | Unemployment levels | | Regulations on foreign ownership of assets |
| Lifestyle | Internet availability | Currency convertibility | | Strength of opposi-tion groups |
| Religious beliefs | Telecommunication infrastructure | Wage levels | | Trade regulations |
| Attitudes toward foreigners | Computer hacking technology | Nature of competition | | Protectionist sentiment |
| Literacy level | New energy sources | Membership in regional economic associations—e.g., EU, NAFTA, ASEAN | | Foreign policies |
| Human rights | | Membership in World Trade Organization (WTO) | | Terrorist activity |
| Environmentalism | | Outsourcing capability | | Legal system |
| "Sweatshops" | | Global financial system | | Global warming laws |
| Pension plans | | | | Immigration laws |
| Health care | | | | |
| Slavery | | | | |

Figure 1. External Factors in international environment
Wheelen & Hunger 2002

One of the factors which is very important in the geographical difference and export is the socio-cultural difference between the country of destination and the country of origin. Culture is one of the most challenging elements of international marketing.

Culture is the "patterns of behavior" and thinking that people living in social groups learn, create and share. Culture distinguishes one human group from another. People's culture includes beliefs, behavioral rules, language, rituals, art, technology, clothing style, food production and cooking methods, religion, customs.

Cultural awareness among international businessmen is not as strong and solid as marketing experts. Today, companies that go global with their products have to contend with local companies that have extensive knowledge of how local people react to a particular cultural pulse. Therefore, new entrants must ensure that their products and advertising techniques are close to people's cultural values in order to leave a good impression of their brand on people's minds. Cultural awareness must be applied in every aspect of marketing: in sales, label printing, advertising. It covers the language, lifestyle and behavioral patterns of the people in the target country. Of course, the company should print in the local language.

Knowing customer preferences is an important issue when it comes to the size of your product offering. It depends on the local cultures as well as the amount of consumption of the regional consumers. For example, in Asian countries, cereal is not a desirable option for breakfast, so there is not much incentive to produce it in large portions. This is also not a smart move to push products into the local culture. When testing new markets with new products, there is always the risk of taking a loss, so you should always do your homework when it comes to culturally influenced preferences.

International managers must understand this system. They should pay attention to the role of culture in international marketing in order to achieve success, and in this regard, they need real and interpretative knowledge of culture. An international marketer must deeply study the specific culture of the country in which the company intends to operate. So cultural elements must be analyzed. When a company decides to go international, it must analyze the target market. This analysis includes micro and macro environments.

What factors should be studied in socio-cultural factors? The important elements of sociocultural that must be studied for having successful export are 16 factors;

1. Customs, norms, values
2. Language
3. Demographics
4. Life expectancies
5. Social institutions
6. Status symbols
7. Lifestyle
8. Relegious beliefs
9. Attitudes toward foreigners

10. Literacy level

11. Human rights

12. Environmentalism

13. Sweatshops

14. Pension plans

15. Health care

16. Slavery

In the following, each of the items and its impact on export innovation will be discussed

.

# 1-1.   Customs, norms, and values

Figure 2 Customs, norms, and values
(https://www.worldatlas.com)

Customs, norms, and values can influence the reaction to the product. For example, colors represent different symbolic concepts in different cultures. A company using yellow flowers in its logo or on the packaging of a product is well received in the United States, but it is a disaster in Mexico, where a yellow flower symbolizes death or disrespect.

In the United States, green color means freshness and health, and in countries that are covered with dense forests, it conveys the concept of illness. Green is the favorite color of Arabs and is used as a forbidden color in a part of Indonesia. In Japan, green represents superior technology. But in America, green electronic devices will not be sold. In Egypt, green is the national color. And it should not be used in the packaging of goods. An English bank wanted to expand its activities in Singapore, and green and blue colors were used in the trademark of this bank. The market research clarified that green represents death in this country and the bank was forced to change itself slowly.

Black is the color of mourning for many countries, but white is the color of mourning for some Asian countries. In Brazil, purple is considered a mourning color, in Mexico it is yellow, and in Ivory Coast, dark red.

In America, blue is considered a masculine color, while in France and Britain, red is more masculine. Pink color is mostly considered a feminine color in America. While, in many other countries yellow color is more feminine, in China red color is a sign of good fortune and good luck.

An international marketer should be familiar with these cultural patterns in the field of color in order to plan optimally in the field of product packaging and advertising. In a foreign market, the choice of colors should be based on the aesthetics of the buyer's culture, not the seller's culture. An international company must understand this difference in values and attitudes within the country and the destination country.

A country whose people's values and beliefs are different from the values and beliefs of the destination country can cause misunderstandings and even costly business failures. All social behaviors are realized in a specific context and are deeply related to other values and beliefs. This means that the mismanagement of cultural differences has high risks. Neglecting or misdirecting these differences can be a misinterpretation of cross-border alliance capabilities, inevitable mistakes in marketing and advertising, and failure to create sustainable sources of competitive advantages. But when cultural differences are successfully managed, they can lead to creative business operations and sustainable sources of competitive advantage.

## 1-2. Languege

Figure 3. Different langueges (https://bilingua.io/)

Language can be verbal or non-verbal. Verbal refers to the way words are said (tone of voice) and non-verbal includes gestures, body posture, and eye contact. It is very important to understand how people in your target market use language. Language in international business is not just learning the language and words, but the language should be along with the culture of the destination country. Language is a big part of culture which are deeply related. In some cases, as culture affects language, and some cases language also affects culture. In order to fully learn a language, you must also understand and learn the culture of the people who speak that language.

Getting to know the culture of the destination country will help you use their language with a new insight in international marketing and brand and export and makes you gain a deeper understanding of the meaning of words and terms and helps you communicate more easily and better with the marketers and customers of the destination country.

Unless you know the culture of the destination country, you cannot market effectively, you cannot choose the right brand, and you cannot export successfully. The language of a country largely depends on the views, values and customs of its people. In fact, the language reflects the values and beliefs of a culture.

The difference between the two cultures is well reflected in their languages. Skill and mastery in subtleties and small differences in a language means to understand that people grew up in two countries and with two different languages, with completely different values and beliefs. You need to prepare your marketing team to understand and accept these differences. Differences in values and beliefs can show themselves in different situations. It is enough to take a look at the slang terms and expressions of different cultures to understand what issues are important in each society.

No matter what culture you look at, you cannot ignore its history. Understanding the history of any culture allows you to understand why certain ideas, beliefs, and values were formed in that culture and why certain words and phrases exist in a language. The history of culture explains where the power that a word or a belief has in language comes from. It also explains the reason for the existence of certain language components. Studying the history of the destination country's language can help international marketers better understand the meaning of words and expressions that have their roots in the same country, as well as words that entered the language of that country from other languages.

Knowing the history of a culture is not only a way to understand better and more, but also shows how words have changed and evolved to reflect the current state of the culture. As an international marketer, you must follow the changes in the meaning of words. Words change in different countries and cultures. A word may have a different meaning years ago than it does now. If we take a brief look at the world of "Etymology", we will realize that words that had a special meaning in the past have a completely different meaning today.

Before the invention of the Internet, it was almost impossible to instantly and quickly define new meanings for words. The analysis, and autopsy of the original meaning of the words was done slowly, and over time and by using them in different situations, their meanings were also defined. Today we can read more and better about it through the internet.

Words can be changed in different ways. Sometimes they are born as simple and innocuous expressions and later become known as profanity or obscene speech. A word like "bimbo", which has Latin roots and is derived from the Italian word "bambino", means child. In the English language, this word is said to a mature man who has a low IQ, but over time it was used to refer to an attractive woman, which, of course, is not polite and is more of a street idiom. Now pay attention to the word *"awesome"*, which is used to describe the best today. The root of the word *"awe"* is synonymous with "dread". This word kept its meaning and negative charge until the 70s and after that people used this word to describe the best things.

There is a popular story about Chevrolet Motor Company's expansion into the Latin American market. According to the story, when Chevrolet introduced its popular "Nova" model to the predominantly Spanish-speaking country, the vehicle sold very poorly. Apparently, it was because "No Va" translates to "It doesn't go" in Spanish. And who wants to buy a car whose name proudly proclaims that it doesn't run?

Branff Airlines, an American airline that closed its doors in 1982, made a similar mistake. When they decided to promote leather seats they showed it in the first class cabins. Their slogan was "Fly in Leather", a harmless phrase in the English language. In Spanish, this phrase is translated as "Vuela en cuero". But what they didn't understand were the sounds of "en cuero" which is exactly the same as "en cuero" which means "naked". Needless to say, "fly naked" wasn't really the message Branff expected to get out.

Although all of these examples are fun to laugh at, they all raise an important point. When doing business in other countries it is important to consider the local language and culture of every aspect of marketing. Companies need to translate website and mobile app content clearly, not just word for word, but to fit the local way of speaking.

Our ever-changing culture forces our language to change as well. Usually, we don't understand the sudden and strange methods and events to change the meaning of a word until we look up its meaning in a dictionary or the Internet or a native English speaker points out these changes.

Now the question that arises is, what is the effect of understanding the characteristics of language on international marketing and export?

More than any other issue, learning the culture and characteristics of the language will help you be more careful in choosing words, whether in international marketing, packaging, or brand definition. Knowing the culture behind any language helps you understand the negative or positive charge of words, especially when the words have no equivalent in your language. If it is otherwise, choosing and using a wrong word in marketing or the word brand may cause misunderstanding and cause failure in international marketing and sales of your products and create a bad situation for your products and company.

Imagine a language like Japanese. The Japanese do not only have an official and informal language, but respect and humility also have their own words and phrases in their language.

When you design an advertising slogan for your brand, pay attention to how this message is perceived in different parts of the world? A phrase that can make your brand very famous in one place can have a very negative effect on your brand in another. For example, the "Pepsi" brand designed the slogan "Pepsi brings you back to life" over time. But this slogan in China was interpreted as "Pepsi brings your ancestors out of the grave". You can probably guess that this interpretation of the Pepsi slogan had a negative effect on this brand in China because of considering the respect of the Chinese people for their ancestors. So if you think you might want to globalize your brand one day, it is better to anticipate these problems from the beginning and prevent them from occurring.

When you learn the culture and history of the

destination country, you can use it effectively in international marketing and branding and exporting your products, then the words will gain new weight and value, and the words that seem incomprehensible and strange, would get more meaning and concept.

## 1-3.  Demographics

Figure 4 Demographics
(https://corporatefinanceinstitute.com)

Demographics is the study of populations. A cognitive demographic analysis looks at a population to reveal that population and its characteristics of families, average education level, average age, income level, ethnic distribution, and other characteristics. Demographic analysis is useful in international business planning because it describes the population in which the business is located.

Those companies that analyze exactly the demographic characteristics of the international market of the destination country get access to good opportunities. For example, the Chinese government passed laws limiting the number of children per family to one child in order to control the rapid growth rate of the country's population. Children's toy marketers paid particular attention to one consequence of these laws and regulations, which was that children in China are becoming morally sensitive and picky. Children in China, who are known as "little emperors", faced a shower of chocolates and computers. which is the result of what became known as "six pocket syndrome". In other words, up to six groups of adults included parents, grandparents, grandparents, uncles and aunts in order to fulfill the wishes of each child which caused Japanese, Danish, and other companies to enter this market.

The age composition of each country's population has made each group need certain goods and services and prefer certain media and retail over others. This helps international marketers what they offer to their target markets. Each demographic group has its own specific needs and purchasing habits. Several foods, clothing and furniture manufacturing companies have targeted their promotional products towards one or more of these groups. However, marketers should be careful not to overgeneralize about ethnic racial groups. Within each racial group, there are consumers who are so different from each other that they differ from Americans who have a European background. According to Macabenta, whose advertising agency specializes in the Filipino market: There really is no such thing as an Asian foreign market. He emphasizes that five main groups of Asian Americans have their own market characteristics. That is, they speak their own language, eat different food, have their own religion and enjoy a completely separate national culture.

Another example is gender and gender roles. Many cultures recognise only male and female genders, and have assumptions about what a man or a woman should be, or do: how to behave, what to wear, what kinds of work they can do. "Men are strong" and "women are caring" are two examples of cultural assumptions about gender. People who don't match up to the assumptions may be judged negatively.

The older group is more important because it is growing rapidly and has not only had the resources but also the time to use them. Women live longer than men, and for this reason their share in the population of elderly groups increases. Research shows that older women don't feel comfortable being forced to choose products that are generally designed for the younger segment. Racial groups are growing rapidly and support all companies and industries. For example, the Asian-American group currently makes up 7 million of the United States population, and is growing rapidly with unique needs.

The effect of all these changes and developments is the fragmentation of the mass market and its transformation into a large number of niche markets that differ in terms of age, gender, ethnic and racial background, education level, lifestyle, geographical location, etc. Nowadays, companies are increasingly preparing their products and marketing plans for retail markets. Demographic trends in the short and medium term can be trusted.

## 1-4. Life expectancy

Figure 5 Life expectancy (https://www.upstate.edu)

Life expectancy (LE) is a statistical measure

of the average time an organism (in our case human) is expected to live, based on the year of its birth, its current age and other demographic factors including gender. There are great variations in life expectancy between different parts of the world, mostly caused by differences in public health, medical care, and diet. Comparing life expectancies from birth across countries can be problematic. There are differing definitions of live birth versus stillbirth even among more developed countries, and less developed countries often have poor reporting.

Worldwide, the average life expectancy at birth was 71.5 years, 68.4 years for males and 72.8 years for females over the period 2010–2015 according to United Nations World Population Prospects (UN Population Prospects, Revised 2015).

In the United States, African-American people have shorter life expectancies than their European-American counterparts. For example, white Americans born in 2010 are expected to live until age 78.9, but black Americans only until age 75.1. In contrast, Asian-American women live the longest of all ethnic groups in the United States, with a life expectancy of 85.8 years. The life expectancy of Hispanic Americans is 81.2 years (Center for Disease Control, CDC, 2019).

Overall, the United States ranks 49 globally in LE. The highest life expectancy is found in Monaco (Europe) and the lowest life expectancy is found in Angola (Africa) ("Life Expectancy", 2019). Ranking 49 in the world in life expectancy doesn't sound so bad when you consider over 200 countries contribute data but it is problematic and concerning given the comparative abundance of resources of the United States. Some argue that the United States, with access to health sciences, technology, and supported innovation should be a global leader in life expectancy rates with a much higher global ranking.

As life expectancy increases, people will change to products and services. Therefore, it is better for international marketers to study the life expectancy rate of the destination country rather than the more expensive products and services for the destination country.

## 1-5. Social institution

Figure 5 Social institution

A social institution is an established practice, tradition, behavior, or system of roles and relationships that is considered a normative structure or arrangement within a society. The five major social institutions in sociology are family, education, religion, government (political), and the economy.

The family is one of the most important social institutions. It is considered a "building block" of society because it is the primary unit through which socialization occurs.

Friedrich von Hayek, one of the geniuses of Austrian economics and philosopher, says that the family is considered the most important pillar of society in the modern world, which plays a decisive and important role in human freedom. He states that if the institution of the family becomes weak, freedom will be lost. Hayek argues that in today's democratic and modern society, the thing that prevents the state from becoming a state and the cultivation of communist thoughts among people is the family. For example, people whose views are formed in an environment like school will have similar views because schools only teach one particular type of ideology; and if there is no family, all people will have the same way of thinking and lose their free thinking.

The family is the oldest social institution in the society and it is also the institution that is closest to the social space while having the closest relationship with the individual space. In fact, family is a bridge between individual and social space, which has many common features with each of these spaces. Economically, the family is also a central institution; not only because historically the family has been the source of production and distribution, but also because the institution of the family is the most important communicator of social ideas. Therefore, the study of the family institution has a special relationship with the study of culture. Although mainstream economics had largely neglected the role of the family as well as the role of culture in determining economic outcomes, such practice changed over time and economists also investigated the role of the family institution and cultural issues in determining economic outcomes. Economists have acknowledged that it is important to include the family in economic analyzes in order to examine micro and macro phenomena, from fertility rates to unemployment cycles.

Natalie Bau and Raquel Fernandez, in their article titled "The Family as a Social Institution", explain how culture and the family interact with each other and examine this interaction in four ways. First of all, they address the fact that diverse family institutions exist around the world and have existed throughout history. In the first part of their article, they describe the changes of the family institution over time and in different regions of the world, and then they provide an explanation for these variations and changes. In the next section, they outline some family choices that relate to intergenerational sustainability and family economics. The main focus of this section is on decisions such as having children and women's labor force participation, which have significant consequences for both the status of women and the economy. The third part of the article is related to the effects of cultural traditions determined by the family, such as dowry, polygamy and living with the spouse's family. In particular, they show how traditions and patterns of marriage and preference for sons affect economic and social components, including investment in human capital, fertility patterns, and partner violence. The last part of the article also explains how cultural change affects the family institution and the status of different family members. Therefore, international marketers should study about the family in the destination country and the changes that have occurred in the family during times so that they can market and export their products and services based on their needs.

John J. Macionis defined education as "The social institution through which society provides its members with important knowledge, including basic facts, jobs, skills, cultural norms and values."

Every country in the world has some kind of advanced education system, but these systems, as well as the educational values and philosophies of those who manage these systems, are very different. In general, the wealth of a country is directly proportional to the quality of its education system. For example, in the poor, education may be seen as a luxury good that the rich can afford, while in the rich, education is accessible to a wider range of people. This is because in the poorer, money is spent on more pressing needs such as food and shelter, reducing financial and time investments in education (Little & McGivern, 2016).

It is important for international companies to know about a country's education system. The level and nature of education can have a major impact on how much consumers spend on external marketing activities.

Religion is another social institution that plays a significant role in society. It is an organized system of beliefs and practices designed to fill the human need for meaning and purpose (Durkheim, 1915). According to Durkheim, "Religion is a unified system of beliefs and practices relative to sacred things, that is to say, things set apart and forbidden."

The government is another social institution that plays a vital role in society. It is responsible for maintaining order, protecting citizens from harm, and providing for the common good. The government does this through its various sub-institutions and agencies, such as the police, the military, and the courts. These legal institutions regulate society and prevent crime by enforcing law and policy. The government also provides social services, such as education and healthcare, ensuring the general welfare of a country or region's citizens.

Economy is a social institution that is responsible for the production and distribution of goods. It is also responsible for paying money and other resources. The economy is divided into three sectors: the primary sector, the secondary sector and the tertiary sector. The sector includes all industries that deal with production and production of natural resources, agriculture, forestry, fishing and mining. The secondary sector includes all industries that deal with the conversion of raw materials into finished products such as manufacturing and construction. The third sector is all industries that provide services to people, including education, health care, and tourism (Little and McGivern, 2016).

## 1-6. Status Symbol

Status symbols come regularly as a result of occasions in history and advancements in culture as well as other shifting financial variables. Each nation and culture is diverse and as a result you'll regularly see status symbols significantly varying around the world. Other variables such as age, sex and calling have an impact on what individuals consider being symbols of status. Be that as it may, in this brief diagram, we are going be looking at a few of the more common or well known status images around the world.

For example, in Africa, status symbols can exceptionally a parcel depending on locale and social status around Africa. Within the more well off ranges of Africa, especially South Africa, innovation and cars tend to be the foremost noticeable status symbols and the ones that everybody competes for.

Costly cars, motorbikes, Blackberries and shrewd phones are all considered to be status symbols, with flashier brands being the ones that are most wanted. The impact of the items you claim and their impact on your standing is dependent to a great extent on how much they fetched instead of how they might advantage your life.

In zones of financial battle, where the lion's share of individuals cannot manage these sorts of extravagances, status symbols are exceptionally distinctive. In West Africa, in Mauritania, sufficiently measured ladies are respected as images of tall social status for their spouses. Having a stout spouse is thought to show riches since a spouse must be able to manage sufficient nourishment to keep her well-fed at her noteworthy measure. This social marvel, in any case, has had unsafe impacts and there are a few charitable social orders in Africa battling to alter this tradition.

Since there is such an assortment of societies inside Asia, there are numerous diverse status symbols to be found. In Malaysia and Thailand, braces are considered to be an in vogue adornment and an image of riches and numerous youngsters have fake braces connected to their teeth. In China, buying shape specific brands is a sign of status and riches, much like it is in other nations. In any case, it isn't fair architect dress and sports cars that they consider to be symbols of status. Starbucks, for case, is considered to be an extravagance brand due to the comparatively tall costs of their items and the company's internationality. In expansion to this, in later a long time status symbols have begun to move absent from the standard and the Chinese affluent are trying to find commodities that are costly however exceptional, such as purebred Tibetan Mastiffs, which can offer for $1million per dog.

Somewhere else around Asia, outlandish creatures are status symbols, especially extraordinary cats such as cheetahs and lions. Youthful tycoons will regularly take selfies with their costly pets with as numerous signs of riches as conceivable display within the picture, like speedboats extravagance cars and their luxurious homes.

Whereas the larger part of affluent western nations still holds to conventional status symbols – like costly tech, vehicles and properties – another slant has come around in later a long time that has seen the upper levels of society seeking after 'guilt-free' joys. A solid way of life, for case may be a symbols of status and cash is regularly going through on items and administrations that are ecologically inviting and common. Numerous individuals with nonessential salary select to spend it on costly natural nourishments, work out gear and administrations that can go towards supporting one's physical or otherworldly wellbeing. None of these, be that as it may, come cheap and investing more cash on these items and administrations is seen to demonstrate your riches as well as your devotion to wellbeing and wellness.

There's another side to this sort of western status symbols that the west has in common with Japan and an extend of other nations. Efficiency is seen as a symbols of status and experts are considered to be more proficient depending on how difficult they work. In Japan, falling sleeping at your work area is seen as a great thing in some occasions because it demonstrates how difficult you've got been working and the larger part of American CEOs revere a work-centred lifestyle, working as numerous as 100 hours and more per week. This can be regularly a result of social mind-set and in both Japanese and American culture, being lazy is considered to be a lamentable quality within the working world and it is to some degree anticipated of experts to create their work their primary need in life.

## 1-7. Lifestyle

The lifestyle of customers is very important for international marketers. They try to offer better products and implement better advertising campaigns and promotional programs by researching the lifestyle of their target groups. In fact, lifestyle is a specific and observable way of living. This way of life is reflected in the goods and services that customers use, in their behavioral habits and other characteristics that are "visible".

Figure 7 Lifestyle

People's lifestyle and social class affects their purchase intention by influencing their beliefs and attitudes and separates different people from each other and makes them different and distinct. In fact, lifestyle is a reflection of consumer choices and how to spend one's income. The concept of lifestyle has a high place in the literature of social sciences, and many famous scientists in this field, including the famous German sociologist Max Weber, have discussed it. Max Weber has discussed its concept in his study of social classes.

In general, lifestyle refers to people's choices about their activities that show the way they want to live. 3 very important factors affect the lifestyle:

1- The way people have grown up.

2- Their personal interests and values.

3- Expectations that the world around people has from them.

In one study, when rich people and poor people were asked about their values and valued activities, they all mentioned sports and reading and learning without exception, but for the rich, these were the first to fifth priorities, and for the poor, almost No priority and in the last ranks! The issue of people being different in terms of their priorities and the time and money they spend is an attractive issue that has spread to international marketers as well. Consumers choose products because they are more closely related to their desired lifestyle. Based on these differences, international marketers divide the market of the destination country and then prepare their marketing mix for that sector.

AIO is a well-known framework for defining consumer lifestyles that gives marketers a new insight into consumer behavior. This framework states that everyone's lifestyle is a combination of Activities, Interests and Opinions. Activities refer to the manner in which the consumer spends his or her time. These activities move in the direction of consumer interests. For example, one's activities move towards work and social activities, which are reflected in more special interests such as food, family, and media habits. For example, which social media does a person spend most of his time on, and which media does he refer to for information about the outside world? For meals, do you prefer a warm home-cooked meal or, on the contrary, do you prefer wandering around new restaurants and eating food you've never eaten before?

Opinions refer to a person's opinion about himself, others, the society he lives in, and the future. For example, are others trustworthy and can they be trusted, or are others fundamentally untrustworthy? Is there a bright and promising future waiting or on the contrary, every day will be worse than yesterday?

Therefore, consumers choose their lifestyle and try to achieve their desired lifestyle by purchasing specific products and brands. This behavior creates many opportunities in international markets and these differences can be important for international marketers and their exports. By considering these differences, international marketers can send a product and service to the international market that is exactly suited to the consumer's lifestyle.

# 1-8. Relegius belifs

Figure 6 Religion belifs

Many international companies ignore the influence of religion, but it is important to distinguish between shared beliefs for example, in Islam, Buddhism or Christianity. The international marketing manager must be aware of the religious divisions in the active countries. In an Islamic country, people do not show interest in products that are considered non-Sharia from the point of view of their religion, and in such cases, religion makes it difficult to supply a product in an Islamic country, and the international market has an impact on its sale. An example of the influence of religious beliefs in international marketing is the ban on the production of pork products and alcoholic beverages in the Middle East. However, if a product is accepted or emphasized by religion in these Islamic countries, the desire of the people of the Islamic nations will increase and cause more demand and supply, and as a result, a positive effect on the international market. So, religion as one of the important parameters can affect the success rate of international markets and the production and supply of international companies.

Religiosity, spirituality and religion have an effect on the attitudes, views, decisions and finally on the behavior of international consumers. Many researches have confirmed the effect of religiosity on the purchase intention. Religious tendencies play an important role in Islamic countries like Iran, where Islamic thoughts and tendencies prevail, and the product that will be offered in the future in this market, if it conflicts with the religious beliefs of the people. If it is, it may lose its credibility as well as the loyalty of customers. In predominantly Muslim countries such as Malaysia, the level of religious commitment among individuals is high and therefore, it is likely that we will see the influence of religion on consumer purchasing behavior. Today, religious and activist groups widely use the method of boycott to punish their target countries. For example, the policies of the United States in the Middle East and Afghanistan have caused many Muslim countries to ask consumers not to buy their products and services. Banning some brand names in Muslim countries clearly shows their religious sensitivity in the selection of western brands.

## 1-9. Attitude toward foreign

Much research relating to consumer attitudes toward foreign products, and foreign investment has been conducted in diffrent countries. While some consumers prefer global or forcign products and view them as symbols of status, others exhibit strong preferences for domestic-made products and have negative attitudes towards foreign or imported products. Such negative attitudes towards foreign products can arise from a number of sources.

ATTITUDE

Figure 9 Attitude toward foreign

Consumers may think products from certain countries are of inferior quality, hold feelings of animosity toward a country, or consider it wrong, almost immoral, to buy foreign products. Foreign products are more likely to be evaluated positively when there is no perceived domestic alternative, and hence no other point of reference for evaluating products. By understanding what the country of origin can have or how it affects people's purchase decision, we should look at branding with a fresh look in all industrial and commercial sectors.

The image of a country does not only affect the political parts of a country; this issue can drag the economy of a society to the point of destruction.

## 1-10. Literacy level

You have cultural literacy when you know what an average member of that culture would be expected to know, which is usually assumed and often unstated (Hirsch, 1983). Hirsch (1983) developed the term "cultural literacy" because people can't learn reading, writing, and other communication as skills separate from the culturally assumed knowledge that shapes what people communicate about.

Figure 7 Literacy level
https://www.participatelearning.com/

For example, the meaning of many words is culture-specific. Telling someone you wear thongs to the beach in Australia is common, but it would have a very different reaction in the USA! Cultural literacy is culture-specific. There are too many different cultures to be literate in all of them. Most people have a fluent cultural literacy in their culture of origin, as they will have been learning their culture's assumed knowledge from childhood. You will need to develop new cultural literacies when you enter a new culture, or interact with members of that culture.

## 1-11. Human rights

Figure 11 Human rights
https://www.greenbiz.com/

Human rights are ethical standards or norms for certain measures of human conduct and are frequently ensured in metropolitan and worldwide law. They are commonly caught on as inalienable, principal rights "to which an individual is intrinsically entitled basically since she or he could be a human being" and which are "inalienable in all human beings", notwithstanding of their age, ethnic beginning, area, dialect, religion, ethnicity, or any other status. They are applicable all over and at each time within the sense of being universal, and they are populist within the sense of being the same for everyone. They are respected as requiring sympathy and the run the show of law and forcing a commitment on people to regard the human rights of others, and it is by and large considered that they ought to not be taken absent but as a result of due prepare based on particular circumstances. The convention of human rights has been profoundly compelling inside worldwide law and worldwide and countries differ significantly in their respect for and political recognition of human rights.

## 1-12. Envirnmentalism

Figure 8 Environmentalism

Environmentalism, political and ethical movement that seeks to improve and protect the quality of the natural environment through changes to environmentally harmful human activities; through the adoption of forms of political, economic, and social organization that are thought to be necessary for, or at least conducive to, the benign treatment of the environment by humans; and through a reassessment of humanity's relationship with nature. In various ways, environmentalism claims that living things other than humans, and the natural environment as a whole, are deserving of consideration in reasoning about the morality of political, economic, and social policies.

Environmentalism or natural rights could be a wide logic, belief system, andsocial development with respect to concerns for natural security and advancement of the wellbeing of the environment, especially as the degree for this wellbeing looks for to consolidate the affect of changes to the environment on people, creatures, plants and non-living matter. Whereas environmentalism centers more on the natural and nature-related viewpoints of green philosophy and legislative issues, ecologism combines the belief system of social biology and environmentalism. ecologism is more commonly utilized in mainland European dialects, whereas environmentalism is more commonly utilized in English but the words have marginally diverse connotations.

Environmentalism signifies a social development that looks for to impact the political handle by campaigning, activism, and instruction in arrange to secure characteristic assets and ecosystems. A naturalist may be an individual who may talk out around our common environment and the feasible administration of its assets through changes in open approach or person conduct. This may incorporate supporting hones such as educated utilization, preservation initiatives, investment in renewable assets, made strides efficiencies within the materials economy, transitioning to unused bookkeeping ideal models such as environmental financial matters, reestablishing and revitalizing our associations with non-human life or indeed selecting to have one less child to decrease utilization and weight on resources. In different ways (for case, grassroots activism and challenges), earthy people and natural associations look for to grant the common world a more grounded voice in human affairs.

# 1-13. Sweatshops

Figure 9 Knit-goods sweatshop, Queens, New York, 1997

Sweatshop is a workshop whose working conditions are difficult or dangerous and at the same time its wages are lower than normal. Workers may work long hours without adequate pay regardless of mandatory overtime or minimum wage laws; Child labor laws may also be violated. "Annual General Report in 2006 " of the Factory Inspection Organization, for the compatibility of FLA laws, has examined the situation in 18 countries, including Bangladesh, El Salvador, Colombia, Guatemala, Malaysia, Sri Lanka, Thailand, Tunisia, Turkey, China, India, Vietnam, Honduras, Indonesia, Brazil, Mexico and the United States. Regarding the worst forms of child labor, the Ministry of Labor found that 18 developed countries did not meet the International Labor Organization's recommendation for an adequate number of inspectors.

## 1-14. Pension plans

Figure 10 Pension plans

In the latest report of the OECD organization, the pension systems in the member countries were reviewed between September 2015 and September 2017, which resulted in a decrease in pensions compared to previous years. Making changes in the retirement age, benefits, insurance rights or contributions from the tax rate in countries including pension reforms are considered.

Like various countries, the Czech Republic, Finland, Greece and Poland have done a lot in the field of pension system reforms, and some countries have slightly changed their previous reforms. For example, changing the retirement age is a law that was changed two years ago in six countries. After the member changed the amount of his insurance premium and like others, they changed the amount for all retirees or some retirees.

Pension reforms have had a great impact on the pension systems of countries, especially Canada, the Czech Republic, Finland, Greece and Poland. Among the OECD members,

Indonesia implemented major reforms in this area in the last two years by introducing a plan in the form of Mandatory Development (DB).

Also, in many member countries such as Denmark, Finland, Italy, the Netherlands, Portugal and the Slovak Republic, the average retirement age, taking into account the increase in life expectancy, so that the average retirement age for men is 1.5 years and for women be 2.1.

According to this report, the retirement age in the three countries of Denmark, Italy and the Netherlands will reach 68 years by 2060. This means that the retirement age for professional work in France, Greece, Luxembourg, Slovenia and Turkey is less than 65 years. This number is 59 years for women in Turkey, 60 years in Luxembourg and 74 years in Slovenia.

The report also shows that with the expansion of the aging population in the world, great inequality in working age and changes in the nature of work, the concern about the financial sustainability of the retirement system and retirement income is increasing, and this concern remains in many countries.

Alternative ratings are also different in different countries, for example, in Mexico and Poland it is less than 40% and in Denmark and the Netherlands it is more than 100%. Also, non-OECD countries such as South Africa have a very low predicted net replacement rate, and on the other hand, the future net replacement rates in Argentina, China and India are higher than 8%.

In many members of this organization, pension systems provide people with the possibility of working and retiring at the same time. In European countries, 10% of people aged 64 to 64 or 65 to 69 combine working life and retirement, and about 50% of people over 65 in OECD member countries work part-time, which is in 15 last years has been constant.

Income restrictions imposed in Australia, Denmark, Greece, Japan, Korea and increased investment in pensions. In France, working pensioners have the option to waive their pensions in order to be exempted from paying excess pension taxes despite paying insurance premiums.

In many countries, postponing retirement increases pensions. In Estonia, Iceland, Japan, Korea and especially Portugal, there are many financial incentives for working after retirement, and these incentives are increasing day by day. The countries of Chile, Czech Republic, Estonia, Italy, Mexico, Norway, Portugal, Slovakia and Sweden have proposed the Republic of Acceptance pension as a pension reform.

More than 100% increase the retirement age, which increases financial stability, increases the amount of insurance premiums paid, and reduces retirement costs. In the past two years, 300,000 people have increased their retirement age, bringing Denmark's retirement age to 68 by 2018. Also, Finland will raise the retirement age from 63 years to 65 years and three months. In the Netherlands, the retirement age will increase to 67 years and three months by 2022, but the Czech Republic increased the retirement age from 65 years.

In addition, in France, changes are made in the rules for calculating the amount of population, according to which the amount of payment for full retirement has been increased for one year. The retirement age in Iceland, Israel and Norway is 67 years and in France and Greece is less than 65 years. Regularly in OECD member countries, the normal retirement age for men has increased from 64.3 years to 65.8 years and for women from 63.4 to 65.5 years.

Many pension reforms have been carried out in the last two years in various fields. Twelve OECD countries, including Australia, Canada, Hungary and Latvia, have changed contribution rates or limited eligibility by age or income. 12 other countries such as Canada, Finland, France and Greece have also changed the benefit levels for certain groups or retirees.

Also, 7 countries, including Germany, Greece and the Slovak Republic, have changed the laws related to pension conditions or income conditions, two countries have changed the basic pension conditions according to the position, and seven countries, such as Ireland, have changed the financial incentives. And countries such as Japan and Turkey have also increased five pension coverage ranges.

## 1-15. Healthcare

Figure 15 Healthcare
(https://www.dreamstime.com)

There are many philosophies shaping healthcare services around the world. The USA does not have a universal, free healthcare program, unlike most other developed countries. Instead, in line with the free-market-virtue mindset, most Americans are served by a mix of publicly and privately funded programs and healthcare systems. Most hospitals and clinics are privately owned, with about 60% being non-profits, and another fifth being for-profit facilities. Coverage by federal and state programs is partial, and most insured Americans have employment-based private insurance.

The UK healthcare system covers the whole population via the National Health System (NHS), which is 79% publicly financed from taxes, and operated by the Department of Health. About 20% is paid for by national insurance, and private patients and copayments make up the rest. The UK NHS provides free healthcare for all and higher life expectancy than in the USA, at half the cost. Patient satisfaction is relatively high, at 61%, compared to 29% in the US.

Each country in the EU has its own healthcare system. However, EU members generally share the same goal as the UK model. All healthcare systems in Europe automatically include all citizens irrespective of paying capacity. Secondly, all are mostly funded by taxes paid by the employer and by the public. Healthcare is free, except for some elective and specialist services. The EU average for healthcare expenditure is about 8% of the GDP, but Cyprus and Latvia are at 3.5%, with other East European nations at 5%. Public spending in this sector typically makes up about 15% of the total government budget.

Singapore uses the 3Ms system: a public statutory insurance system, MediShield Life for large hospital bills, and some high-end outpatient treatments as well, but not primary care, or specialist care at the outpatient level. The premiums are subsidized to help even low-earning people to pay them, and working-age people pay more to allow older people to enjoy lower premiums. Thus, the government, healthcare providers, and patients all share the responsibility for healthcare coverage – a multipayer financing system. While competition and market forces enhance the quality of healthcare, the government strictly regulates the costs when they begin to rise beyond affordable rates. The Ministry of Health also plans for workforce strength, training and land allotment for healthcare facilities, along with preventive health interventions. The system's centralized nature keeps administrative costs low and simplifies procedures. Singapore spends about 4.5% of its GDP on healthcare, about 40% by the government, with 30% being out-of-pocket expenses.

China has almost universal publicly funded medical insurance, with urban employees enrolled in employment-based programs. Others enroll voluntarily, for basic subsidized medical insurance. Comprehensive healthcare is covered, but deductibles and copayments apply. There is also a ceiling on reimbursement. China spends about 6.6% of its GDP on healthcare, with 28% being funded by central and local governments, 28% out-of-pocket, and 44% by public or private insurance, and social health donations. These form part of a medical assistance program for the poor.

India provides universal free outpatient and inpatient care at government clinics and hospitals. States are in charge of organizing their healthcare services. India spends less than 4% of its GDP on healthcare, with a quarter being funded by the public sector. Out-of-pocket payments at private hospitals make up 75% of the total expenditure, in stark contrast to other poor countries.

Australia has a tax-funded universal free public health insurance program, called Medicare. All citizens get free care for public and many physician services and drugs at public hospitals. The total expenditure on healthcare is about 10% of GDP, with 67% being from the public sector. It is jointly run by federal, state and territorial governments, and is among the best in the world.

Sub-Saharan Africa has 13% of the world's population but carries a fourth of the world's disease burden. However, it spends only 1% of the global health expenditure. Only six African countries spend 15% of their budgets on healthcare, and these are yet to achieve universal access to reasonable-quality healthcare.

# 1-16. Slavery

Figure 11 Slave ship during the Trans-Atlantic Slave Trade (https://www.antislavery.org/)

Slavery is known as an economic and social system in which people were considered as the property. This has been around since prehistoric times. In this system, they were captured or killed. In fact, one of the main reasons for the backwardness of the great continent in Africa was the use of slavery.

In the course of the slave trade, in addition to the looting of the material wealth and power of the inhabitants, this continent turned into unbalanced societies without a balanced demographic and cultural structure and alien to its historical heritage. The slave does not receive wages for work and has no right to withdraw from work or not to do it. Historically, during the classical era, ancient Greece was the pioneer of slavery. According to documents in the sixth and fifth centuries BC, 80 thousand slaves lived in Greece. The Roman Empire brought slavery to its peak in the classical era and enslaved all the people of the land. So that physicists, astronomers and engineers also became slaves of the empire.

The conquests of the empires caused the nations to be enslaved. This issue continued until the first attempts were made to abolish slavery. According to some historians, the first attempts to abolish slavery date back to the third century BC, which happened in the area of the Maurya or Maurya empire, in which the sale and purchase of slaves was prohibited, but in modern historiography, 960 AD is the first date of the abolition of slavery, which in That Duke of Venice, Pietro Candiano IV, announced the ban on slavery. Since then, governments around the world have banned the sale and purchase of slaves and the exploitation of slaves. The abolition of slavery continued until the United Nations designated December 2th as the International Day for the Abolition of Slavery in 1949. This international day focuses on eradicating modern slavery, such as human trafficking, sexual exploitation, child marriage and forced labor.

Suppression of nations and forcing them into various forms of slavery by the Romans led to the occurrence of three Roman slave wars, the third slave war being the most famous of them. In the middle ages, slavery continued in England after the collapse of the Roman Empire, and the cities of Chester and Bristol were the main destinations for slave traders to sell slaves. Before the discoveries of Christopher Columbus in the west and Vasco da Gama in the east of the world, one of the Portuguese princes named Henry reached the west coast of the African continent in 1441 during the search to find the sea route to India and captured some men and women. After returning to Portugal, Henry sold his captives in the market of Lisbon and established the trading of human beings as commodities in the market of Lisbon. After this incident, several hundred Africans were captured from their lands and sold in the Lisbon market. In early medieval Europe, slavery became so common that the Catholic Church got into the business. In this way, the slave trade was recognized as a legal profession in Europe. From a historical point of view, the roots of the organized slavery of the 17th and 18th centuries should be sought in the newly born European economy. In these years, the European economy was based on agriculture in the vast lands that were acquired during the discovery of this continent and the colonization of East Asia and India. It should be said that slavery in Europe officially started in the 15th century and became a part of the economy of these countries and gradually took on an organized form. In this trade, there was a network of brokers, adventurers, hunters and slave traders who worked together to provide the labor needed for agriculture in the pastures.

A lot of labor was needed for farming in vast pastures, and the profitability of this work for capitalists depended on the use of cheap labor. For this reason, the Europeans turned to exploiting the people of backward countries in Africa. On the other hand, having vast but uninhabited colonies was not in line with the main goal of the Europeans to acquire as much capital as possible. For this reason, efforts were made to move some residents of European countries to these areas, but these measures could not achieve the goals. It was from this time that the purchase of slaves from backward African tribes and their transfer to new lands was on the agenda, and thus, the slave trade became one of the pillars of the Western economy. In addition to the natives of North America who were of the Indian race, the natives of Haiti and then in the 19th century the natives of Tasmania also suffered the same fate. Many European thinkers and intellectuals were involved in this crime. Charles Darwin wrote about the Tasmanian disasters: At some future period, the civilized races of man will certainly remove the savage races from the earth and replace them.

English historian Derek Curton writes about

this: In 1680, the rich merchants of Bristol, Liverpool and London exported 15 thousand African slaves. Later this number increased. Between 1680 and 1786, England alone captured, transported and sold more than 2 million slaves. In 1791, there were 40 English slave-hunting stations located on the west coast of Africa alone, bearing the name of trading office.

At the end of the 18th century, the English slave traders owned half of the slave trade with a fleet of 200 ships with a capacity of 50,000 slaves. As African slaves were transported to new lands, they were also used to work in mines and plantations built in their own countries. The second half of the 19th century was the peak of slavery in Africa. One of the contemporary historian's writes: In the course of the slave trade, not only the material wealth and human resources of the African continent were plundered, but also the inhabitants of this continent turned into unbalanced societies without a balanced demographic and cultural structure and alienated from their historical heritage. Their political and social values were also destroyed. This is a bigger disaster than human killing and captivity and looting of material wealth, because it destroyed the possibility of regeneration of the African continent for a long time.

From 1760, the slave rebellions started in Jamaica and became a widespread wave of rebellions. The structure of European urban societies also changed in this century, and other governments could not continue their activities without considering public opinion. Since the end of the 18th century, movements against slavery had been formed among the public opinion of the West, and the culmination of these movements in England led to the establishment of the Society for the Abolition of the Slave Trade in London. Until 1807, buying and selling slaves was officially banned in England and America. In this way, the second half of the 19th century can be considered the end of the classical period of slavery, but the phenomenon of slavery did not disappear completely, but changed its shape. Although slavery is illegal today, it is estimated that there were between 12 and 30 million slaves in the world in 2010.

Today, the world is facing a new form of slavery, which is called hidden slavery. One of the most important manifestations of hidden slavery in the current era is sexual slavery. All that has been said shows the main and fundamental role of the slave trade in the development of European countries. However, in the years after the abolition of slavery, extensive efforts were made by Western historians to reduce the severity and heinousness of the slave owners' heinous actions and to introduce slavery as a normal practice at the global level. Patrick Manning, professor of history at the University of Pittsburgh, USA, writes in the book Slavery and African Life: Slavery is an institution that has existed in all or most human societies throughout history. These people try to use the history of ancient Greece and Rome to make slavery appear as a normal and widespread phenomenon.

Slavery is prohibited by the Universal Declaration of Human Rights (1948):

"No one shall be enslaved or held in slavery:

all forms of slavery and the slave trade shall be prohibited."

The definitions of modern slavery are mainly taken from the UN Supplementary Convention (1956), which states: "Debt bondage, serfdom, forced marriage and the provision of children for the exploitation of that child are all forms of acts of slavery and require abolition and decriminalization." » The Forced Labor Convention (1930) defines forced labor as "all work or service obtained from a person under threat of punishment and which the person does not perform voluntarily."

Debt bondage: In this type of slavery, people are forced to work for free to repay their debt after being in debt. Many of these people will never be able to pay off their debt and thus the next generations will be forced into slavery.

Forced labor: when people are forced to work without pay, often through violence or threats. Many of these people are those who are trapped in a foreign country without identification papers and cannot get out.

Hereditary Slavery: When people are born

slaves because their families belong to the "slave" class in society. In this case, the status of "slavery" is passed from mother to child.

Human trafficking: the transportation or trade of human beings from one region to another for slavery.

Child slavery: Children are enslaved as domestic workers and forced laborers—for example, in the cocoa, cotton, or fishing industries—trafficked as laborers or for sexual exploitation, or used as child soldiers.

Early and forced marriage: Women and girls who are forced to marry at a very young age or without their consent.

How many millions of slaves are there in the world? In the 2016 global statistics published by the Walk Free Foundation, it is estimated that about 45.8 million people in 167 countries of the world are in some form of slavery. 58% of modern slaves live in five countries: India, China, Pakistan, Bangladesh and Uzbekistan. In this report, it is stated that North Korea has the highest ratio of slaves to its total population (4.4%). Uzbekistan (4%) and Colombia (1.6%)

are next.

Slavery is more common in countries that produce consumer goods through cheap labor. In terms of the number of people who live in slavery, no other country comes close to India. It is estimated that there are around 18.4 million slaves in India. This figure is 3.4 million in China and 2.1 million in Pakistan. Countries that have been politically stable and have high economic wealth have recorded the lowest rate of slavery. The best countries from this point of view are Canada, Germany, Singapore and the United States respectively.

Slavery also exists in developed countries. For example, the Ministry of the Interior of England has announced that there are about 10,000 to 13,000 slaves in this country, who are mostly employed in the field of prostitution.

According to the latest Global Estimates of Modern Slavery (2022) from Walk Free, the International Labour Organization and the International Organization for Migration:

- ✓ 49.6 million people live in modern slavery – in forced labour and forced marriage

- ✓ Roughly a quarter of all victims of modern slavery are children

- ✓ 22 million people are in forced marriages. Two out of five of these people were children

- ✓ Of the 27.6 million people trapped in forced labour, 17.3 million are in forced labour exploitation in the private economy, 6.3 million are in commercial sexual exploitation, and nearly 4 million are in forced labour imposed by state authorities

- ✓ The Covid-19 pandemic has exacerbated the conditions that lead to modern slavery

- ✓ Migrant workers are particularly vulnerable to forced labour.

# Chapter 2.
# Export
# Innovation

In this chapter, first we start with the question of; Why is cultural awareness important in international marketing and exporting?

Cultural awareness among international businessmen is not as strong and solid as marketing experts. When the East India Company entered and started the spice trade in India in the 17th century, they gave special importance to Indian cultural values to immerse themselves in everything. But maybe the competition was not hard at that time, because the early traders were aware of the potential in their business strategy. Today, companies that go global with their products have to contend with local companies that have extensive knowledge of how local people react to a particular cultural pulse. Therefore, new entrants must ensure that their products and advertising techniques are close to people's cultural values in order to leave a good impression of their brand on people's minds. Cultural awareness must be applied in every aspect of marketing: in sales, label printing, advertising. It covers the language, lifestyle and behavioral patterns of the people in the target country. Of course, the company should print in the local language.

Knowing customer preferences is an important issue when it comes to the size of your product offering. It depends on the local cultures as well as the amount of consumption of the regional consumers. For example, in Asian countries, cereal is not a desirable option for breakfast, so there is not much incentive to produce it in large portions. This is also not a smart move to push products into the local culture. When testing new markets with new products, there is always the risk of taking a loss, so marketers should always do their homework when it comes to culturally influenced preferences.

Helping customers connect with their brand and products is essential, and cultural awareness also plays an important role. If entrepreneurs use and implement their knowledge, it will greatly help in formulating a successful international marketing strategy. International marketing training can help you a lot to succeed in your business!

Due to the differences that exist in different geographical areas, exporting organizations should be available. In fact, the goal of innovation is to identify potential (new) international markets and better (new) ways to serve the target market. As a result, the three basic and primary components of innovative marketing are *being unique*, *being new*, and *being unusual*. When exporting companies observe these three components in their organizational processes and activities, it is possible to achieve the set goals. In the following we explain some business cultures in some countries.

## 2-1 Business culture in China

Customs influence how we think and work. The attitude of people in different cultures causes differences in the way of doing business and advertising. Hsieh in his research paper on culture and export, states that the Chinese are very hard working, very flexible and have different strategies in pricing and product development.

Considering the fact that the Chinese today, in the position of the second largest economy in the world, have taken a major share of international trade, it is very important to gain knowledge of their cultural rules. As you can see, it is better to curb this impulse when doing business with the Chinese. Because the customs of Chinese people are different from what you think.

It is best to keep your cool when dealing with Chinese merchants. The most you can do is use kind and polite words or a faint smile. No matter how grateful you are; Do not bring gifts or tip in restaurants, as gifts are not happily accepted in business with the Chinese. Of course, this is a small part of the culture of the Chinese people that we should know. Official policy in Chinese business etiquette prohibits gifts. People in China usually enter the meeting room in a hierarchical order. So be careful. They assume the first person to walk in the room is the board president!

In the culture and customs of Chinese people in business and daily life, the questions

"Have you eaten?" or "Where have you been?" In other cultures, pleasant and casual questions (such as "How are you?") are considered, so pay attention to these questions and go into detail in your answer! If you have eaten, even if you haven't, simply answer "yes" or simply smile and say "thank you!"

In general, you should respect the specific views of the Chinese. They usually place a special value on tradition, collectivism, community, family, and organizations. If you want to succeed in doing business with the Chinese, you need to adapt yourself to the other party's values and worldview. Also, talk about the uniqueness and luxury of your services or products.

Popular topics that are welcome when visiting are about China: art, scenery, landmarks, weather, and geography. You can mention your travel experiences to other countries and mention your positive impressions as a tourist in China!

Try to avoid political discussions. Chinese people are very sensitive to negative comments. In fact, negative answers are considered impolite. So instead of an outright "no," come up with alternatives like "I'll think about it"/"maybe"/"we'll see what happens."

Similarly, if your Chinese counterparts say "it's not a big problem" or "it's not a serious problem", it usually means that there are still problems or the problems are serious.

Body language and gestures are things you should constantly watch out for when doing business in China and with the Chinese. As mentioned above, you must remain calm and composed. Posture should always be formal and careful as it shows self-control and respect. Be careful what you do with your hands too. Putting your hands in your mouth, biting your nails, taking food out of your teeth, and things like that are considered impolite. You can consider below things;

• Meetings and meals in business

• Dress type: conservative suit. Bright colors of any kind are considered inappropriate.

• Punctuality is critical. Being late is a serious offense in Chinese business culture.

• When the meeting is over, you are expected to leave the meeting before your Chinese counterparts.

• Changing business cards is a common practice, so be sure to bring plenty of business cards!

• Depending on the province where you do business, it is recommended that one side of the business card be in English and the other in Simplified Chinese or Traditional Chinese. Include your professional title, especially if it is important to your business. Also, if your business is the oldest, largest, or has some other prestigious distinction, include it on the card.

• Gold is the color of prestige and prosperity, so if you print your business card with gold ink, it will have that connotation.

• Give your card with both hands and make sure the Chinese side is facing the receiver. Carefully receive your card and examine it for a few moments.

- Do not bring gifts! Official Chinese business etiquette policy prohibits gifts. This gesture is considered a bribe, which is illegal in the country.

- If you are invited to a business meal, you must wait to be seated, as there is a seating protocol based on hierarchy. Do not talk about business during the meal.

- During one meal, 20 to 30 servings can be served, so try not to eat too much at once! The trick is to try one sample of each dish.

- Scorpions, locusts, snake skin, dog meat and blood may be served to you. They are considered delicious and first class foods.

- It is also important to know how much you should eat. Leaving the plate empty means that you have not been given enough food and not touching the food is also insulting.

- Don't panic if everyone starts burping and burping. These are signs of enjoyment while eating.

- If you are invited for a drink, you should go, because it is very important to build a strong personal relationship ("guanxi") throughout your business.

• Your Chinese counterpart may test your ability to drink alcohol, especially "Bai Jiu" (common brand names "Mao Tai" and "Er Guo Tou"); a powerful drink that may be compared to aviation fuel! If you decide to go out for a drink, be sure to eat something beforehand. Otherwise, find a good excuse not to drink. Medical excuses are fine and accepted.

• Tipping is generally considered an insult in China and implies that the recipient needs the money.

• The importance of numbers in Chinese culture

Numbers have different meanings in China. For example, 8 is considered the luckiest number in Chinese culture. If you come across the number 8, consider it a sign of goodwill. 6 is considered as a blessing for growth and evelopment.

4 is a taboo number because it sounds like the word "death" and is considered unlucky. 73 means "burial".and 84 means accident. With a little study in their culture, you will understand what numbers to use in the design of products and their packaging.

## 2-2 Business culture in Geramany

The desire for order is also rooted in German business life. Surprises or jokes are not welcomed. Everything is completely planned in advance and decisions are made in advance, and changes are usually very rare once an agreement is made.

Engineers have a special place in Germany and this can be seen in the success of their automobile industry. Employees at all levels are judged strictly on merit and hard work. The relationship with colleagues and foreigners is more direct and they do not always use politics in it.

In Germany, a handshake is the best form of social etiquette, but physical contact is considered more impolite.

The etiquette of eating with Germans is not much different from other places in the world, except for a few small points that you should observe; Put your hands on the table, but your elbows are not on the table, use cutlery, even sandwiches are served with cutlery. Germans give each other a drink before starting, and if you have gone to a restaurant with your German friend and you don't intend to count, don't compliment him because he may agree to you easily the first time.

The legal structure of Germany and other European countries in international trade is based on several legal principles or rules such as non-discrimination, fair trade liberalization and transparency. Especially Germany emphasizes these principles more. These principles are very closely related. For example, according to the Law of Prohibition of Discrimination and Fair Treatment with Other Participating Countries, special treatment permission is never issued to a developing country, or a country like Germany cannot remove some trade barriers between itself and a specific country, or the reduce price of a specific product. According to the commitments made among the members, including non-discrimination commitments, it will be required to give these concessions to other member countries. Therefore, the removal of the trade barrier will be realized without the need for new negotiations between all members.

Cuntries do not look at the category of export as a specialized professional activity, producers do not have a correct idea of international relations and the issue of export and consider it similar to their domestic sales.

Because they have not seen the necessary training as a guide for exporting to Germany and other countries. For this reason, they expect to be successful in attracting foreign customers only with expensive and aimless stereotypical activities such as participating in international exhibitions, sending group emails, and the like.

It does not mean that one should not participate in the exhibition or not have official communication, but such activities should be in the heart of the specialized and continuous process and not become a temporary, low-benefit and expensive process.

In the end, we should know that although sanctions are sometimes a big obstacle on the way of exports and currency stabilization is one of the most important prerequisites for the realization of plans, but taking informed and open-ended decisions in this situation can make the trade path with other countries smoother. For sure success, use the skills and knowledge of professional and experienced merchants who will be the best guide for exporting to Germany.

# 2-3 Business culture in Canada

In Canada, certain customs govern people's relationships. Of course, due to the regionalism and high cultural diversity of Canada, it is very difficult to introduce a specific behavioral style to establish communication, however, there are some basic communication styles that are largely accepted and standardized throughout the country. In Canada, as long as the relationship between two people is not official, they call each other by their family name and look directly into the other person's eyes when shaking hands. Also, in general, in English-speaking areas it is not customary to interrupt someone else's conversation, but in French-speaking areas, it is more likely that someone will interrupt someone else's conversation.

In Canadian social culture, non-verbal expressions are used only to add emphasis to a message or to be part of a person's unique personal communication style. Canadians also like to talk about their personal lives with friends and colleagues and expect others to be straightforward. The use of academic titles is especially important in Quebec, where two words of respect are used: "Monsieur" and "Madame". Otherwise, use Ms. or Mr. as long as it is not possible to use a first name.

Canadians start meetings with minimal discussion which can be a form of greeting, but in Quebec the culture is slightly different and more time may be spent on greetings. In Canada, meetings are generally well organized and scheduled. Even if the topic discussed in the meeting is an important topic, they tend to discuss it informally and calmly.

In the meetings held by English speakers, there will be a certain degree of democracy and all participants will be involved and participate in the discussions. But in French-speaking meeting etiquette, due to greater respect for hierarchy, discussions may be more focused around senior participants. Business meetings in Canadian companies are spent reviewing proposals, presenting plans, brainstorming and discussing decisions. In these meetings, participants are usually at different levels of work with different experiences, and everyone is expected to express their opinions.

In speeches, when presenting information, it is important to use clear facts and figures to support your claims and promises. Canadians are basically rational people and cannot be persuaded by emotions, passion and excitment.

In the speech culture of the Canadian people,

the speech should be short and clear, focusing on the topic and refrain from using specialized and technical terms. To negotiate, you must first get enough information about the company you want to contact and determine exactly what you want to get from the negotiation. In speeches, when presenting information, it is important to use clear facts and figures to support your claims and promises. Canadians are basically rational people and cannot be persuaded by emotions, passion and excitement.

In the speech culture of the Canadian people, the speech should be short and clear, focusing on the topic and refrain from using specialized and technical terms. To negotiate, you must first get enough information about the company you want to contact and determine exactly what you want to get from the negotiation.

Canada has 2 official languages; English and French. There are language laws in Canada, depending on the province, that require businesses to translate all content and anything the customer encounters into French.

Canada is culturally rooted in its French ancestry, and it is essential that companies to trade with Canada determine their product and provide accurate translation with that in mind. Make no mistake, there are many differences between Canadian French and the French spoken in France. Make sure you work with a professional translation company that uses NATIVE speakers of the target language.

Don't exaggerate product or service features. Honesty is highly valued in Canadian culture. In your meetings to do business with Canada, it is essential that you do not over-promote, exaggerate or lie about the features offered.

The same applies to marketing your products to Canadian citizens. Product promotion with exaggerated benefits and features will limit your chances of profit; because the product has finally reached the hands of the consumers, and when the real quality is determined, they distrust your brand.

Canadians value their cultural identity and do not take kindly to foreigners trying to impose their culture on them. Focus your message on how your product or service will benefit Canadians and how it can be integrated into Canadian identity. Remember that you are a guest in Canada and your success depends on their acceptance.

## 2-4 Business culture in France

Another country like France will be different in export due to different conditions and different culture. The French Republic is one of the countries located in Western Europe, which has many regions and territories across the seas. France is one of the three countries that have coasts on the Mediterranean Sea and the Atlantic Ocean (the other two countries are Spain and Morocco).

In the field of international standards, France can be considered one of the leading countries. High standards of living, education, health, life expectancy, freedom and high human development index introduce France as one of the ideal countries to live.

When talking about France, many people

think of cinema, art and culture, historical monuments and romantic dinners. But this historical country, in addition to the mentioned attractions, is one of the economic poles of Europe. A country that is not only in ideal conditions in terms of human resources, but also in a very positive position in terms of industry and mining infrastructure.

In addition to these, France as the second economic pole of the European Union in the field of important industries such as automobile manufacturing, metalworking, petrochemical, textiles, cosmetics and hygiene etc is active. As a result, the volume of trade of this country in the international arena is considered stunning compared to many European countries. Labor productivity in France is higher than many European competitors; it has even become a model for developing countries. Paying attention to things like industrial psychology, the importance of manpower motivation and developing programs for the well-being and job security of employees in periods of economic austerity are among the most important things that have brought sustainable growth and economic well-being. The so-called in-service training of employees is not developed by the employers, but by the government, on the other hand, the government programs that are provided to train and improve the skills of the workforce help the economy of this country to become knowledge-based and modernized and the human forces operate with the highest level of efficiency.

The business structure in France is hierarchical and decision-making is generally done at the top of the organization. The French like to act independently in politics and business, and negotiating with them may seem more boring than negotiating with other Europeans, Japanese, and Americans. The French are usually steeped in their tumultuous history and have certain norms for everything that separate them from other nations. French norms in democracy, law, government system, military strategies, philosophy, culture, economy, etc. are different from other nations, so there are many issues that should be learned and paid attention to when faced with them.

The French education system is such that most of them do not know much about the culture and geography of other nations, especially small or remote countries, so their attitude towards foreign parties is interestingly neither positive nor negative and does not contain any special prejudice. They enter into a deal with you on the condition that you are a potential buyer of their products or a seller of a good product, and they usually seem kind to you in the initial meeting. If you can't speak French with them, in their subconscious mind they think you are an anglophile (English lover), which is not very desirable in their opinion, but of course, in many cases, you can't do anything!

Most senior managers of French companies are graduates of exemplary schools. These schools create a sense of scientific struggle in their students, which is unique in the world, and it causes the education of a highly educated management population, whose approach to management is accompanied by great scientific precision.

According to the French, management is a

thoughtful work that is associated with detailed analysis, complete mastery of concepts and information, and finally with the implementation of logical decisions. More practical issues such as motivating employees are not considered as much in French management thinking as they are in other countries.

When the decision is made at the senior levels of the organization, it is referred to the management of lower levels for implementation. From the point of view of those who are consensus-oriented and have a non-hierarchical background, this directive approach is very authoritarian and lacks the necessary components for teamwork.

French companies are very strict in functional and hierarchical issues. The senior management alone determines the future direction of the company and in the next stage, this vision is transferred to the lower management levels for implementation. Therefore, as in the countries of Sweden and the Netherlands, senior management tends to make directive decisions instead of collaborative decision-making.

In addition, the concentration of power in the hands of senior management reinforces the centralist approach, which is now evident in many other aspects of French life. Lower levels include different management levels that are organized along functional lines of responsibility.

When things are going well, the hierarchical approach seems very appropriate and effective, but the weakness of this system becomes apparent when a problem arises and there is a need for a quick response. In these situations, it sometimes seems that there is no sense of personal responsibility in doing things.

French business and business behavior emphasizes politeness and formality. Mutual trust and respect are necessary to get the job done, and this trust is created with the right behavior. If you don't know French, a little apology for not speaking French can go a long way in your business relationships.

However, it's not a bad idea to learn a few French words and phrases to show that you're interested in a long-term relationship. Usually, according to the social position, level of education, and the city where a French person grew up, you can predict his style of communication.

The French seem too frank in business, which may be the reason for their carelessness in screwing the other party. The French are impressed by conversational skills that demonstrate a thoughtful understanding of the situation and its implications. It is necessary to make an appointment for the meeting at least 2 weeks in advance. The meeting request can be written or verbal. The meeting time is often set by the secretary. Try not to have your meetings in July and August. These two months are travel and vacation months for the French. If you think you will be late for the meeting, be sure to call and give a reason for your delay. Meetings are held to discuss issues, not to make decisions. Avoid bragging because the French are allergic to it.

The world of business and business in France always emphasizes formality. Wait until they tell you where to sit. Make direct eye contact when you speak. Things move slowly in France, so be patient and don't be put off by the fact that formalities are followed carefully. Do not pressure the other party to achieve the goal. This has the opposite result. The French will check all the details of your offer.

Never be too intimate. If you want to sell something to the French, don't use techniques that put them under too much pressure. If you present your proposal in a logical, complete, and gentle manner, they will be more receptive to it. After reaching an agreement, they may insist that all agreements be written down in a detailed and detailed form in a written contract.

A Frenchman never considers you similar to him and sees you as better as or worse than him, but he always thinks that he is different from a Frenchman. Most of the French, like the Japanese, believe that it is impossible for you to fully comply with their standards and norms.

The most important points about business culture in France are as follows:

• Educational background and mental skills are

important points in France.

- The French government and industry have long had much closer relations than other industrialized countries, which has led to the emergence of many senior government employees who play an important role in the industry.

- Long-term planning has been one of the important principles of the French approach for many decades and has led to the design of detailed plans by companies.

- Most of the big French companies, along with the central tendencies, establish their main offices and centers and large branches in Paris.

- Executive directors of French companies usually have a charismatic personality and lead the company in a dominant and commanding manner.

- French companies tend to have a rigid hierarchy with a clear and progressive decision-making and reporting system.

- Communicating in different levels of the

hierarchy is considered unusual.

- Promotion is done through a set of experience, educational degrees and evident competencies.

- The management style is usually directive by providing guidance and orders in information meetings to employees.

- In open and formal meetings, very few disagreements with the president are evident. Other differences can be seen in the lobbies before the meeting.

- The competition of similar groups can make it difficult to manage cross-functional teams.

# Conclusin

As you have seen, the variety of variety is different due to different weather conditions, social, economic, political, legal, economic, technological factors related to each geographical region, which can affect the type of export of exporting companies. In this book, you learned that before exporting, you should evaluate all these factors in the destination country and create innovations in services, products and packaging based on the culture of that country. For example, if you intend to export to France, you must have detailed information about the social and cultural factors related to that country so that you can effectively export to that country. The focus of this book has been on sociocultural factors.

# Refrences

1) Bau, N., & Fernández, R. (2021). *The family as a social institution* (No. w28918). National Bureau of Economic Research.

2) Durkheim, E. (2006). *Durkheim: Essays on morals and education* (Vol. 1). Taylor & Francis.

3) Healthmanagement.org. (2006). Facts & Figures: The UK Healthcare System. https://healthmanagement.org/c/it/issuearticle/facts-figures-the-uk-healthcare-system

4) Little, W., McGivern, R., & Kerins, N. (2016). *Introduction to sociology-2nd Canadian edition*. BC Campus.

5) Medical.mit.edu (2021). Healthcare in the United States: The top five things you need to know. https://medical.mit.edu/my-mit/internationals/healthcare-united-states

6) Tikkanen, R. et al. (2021). U.S. Health Care from a Global Perspective, 2019: Higher Spending, Worse Outcomes? https://www.commonwealthfund.org/publicati

ons/issue-briefs/2020/jan/us-health-care-global-perspective-2019

7) Great Britain: The National Health Service. https://sites.psu.edu/smithcivicblog/2016/01/16/great-britain-the-national-health-service/

8) Ec.europa.eu (2017). European semester thematic factsheet: Health systems.

9) Thorlby, R. (2021). International Health Care System Profiles England. https://www.commonwealthfund.org/international-health-policy-center/countries/england

10) Earn, L. C. (2021). International Health Care System Profiles Singapore. https://www.commonwealthfund.org/international-health-policy-center/countries/singapore

11) Gupta, I. (2021). International Health Care System Profiles India. https://www.commonwealthfund.org/international-health-policy-center/countries/singapore

12) Earn, L. C. (2021). International Health Care System Profiles Singapore. https://www.commonwealthfund.org/international-health-policy-center/countries/singapore

13) World Health Organization. Regional Office for Europe, European Observatory on Health

Systems and Policies, Miguel Á González Block, Hortensia Reyes Morales, Lucero Cahuana Hurtado. et al. (2020). Mexico: health system review. World Health Organization. Regional Office for Europe. https://apps.who.int/iris/handle/10665/334334

14) Kim, S. Universal Healthcare Systems and Fragmentation in Latin America. https://sites.google.com/macalester.edu/phla/key-concepts/universal-healthcare-systems-and-fragmentation-in-latin-america

15) www.ilo.org. More than 140 million denied access to health care in Latin America and the Caribbean. https://www.ilo.org/global/about-the-ilo/newsroom/news/WCMS_007961/lang--en/index.htm

16) www.un.org/africarenewal. December 2016–March 2017 | Vol. 30 No. 3

17) Fang, H. (2021). China. https://www.commonwealthfund.org/international-health-policy-center/countries/china

18) Blumenthal, D. et al. (2020). Covid-19 — Implications for the Health Care System. The New England Journal of Medicine.

https://www.nejm.org/doi/full/10.1056/nejmsb
2021088

19) Apps.who.int. (2020). Mexico: health system
review.
https://apps.who.int/iris/handle/10665/334334

20) Altman, D. (2020). Understanding the US
failure on coronavirus—an essay by Drew
Altman. The BMJ.
https://doi.org/10.1136/bmj.m3417.
https://www.bmj.com/content/370/bmj.m3417

21) Scally, G. et al. (2020). The UK's public
health response to covid-19.
https://doi.org/10.1136/bmj.m1932.
https://www.bmj.com/content/369/bmj.m1932

22) Ham, C. (2020). The challenges facing the
NHS in England in 2021.
https://doi.org/10.1136/bmj.m4973.
https://www.bmj.com/content/371/bmj.m4973

23) www.thelancet.com. (2020). Building a
resilient NHS, for COVID-19 and beyond.
https://doi.org/10.1016/S0140-6736(20)32035-
3.
https://www.thelancet.com/journals/lancet/arti
cle/PIIS0140-6736(20)32035-3/fulltext

24) Han, E. et al. (2020). Lessons learnt from easing COVID-19 restrictions: an analysis of countries and regions in Asia Pacific and Europe. https://doi.org/10.1016/S0140-6736(20)32007-9. https://www.thelancet.com/journals/lancet/article/PIIS0140-6736(20)32007-9/fulltext

25) Child, J. et al (2020). Collaboration in crisis: Reflecting on Australia's COVID-19 response. https://www.mckinsey.com/industries/public-and-social-sector/our-insights/collaboration-in-crisis-reflecting-on-australias-covid-19-response#

26) Ihekweazu, C. et al. (2020). Africa's response to COVID-19. https://doi.org/10.1186/s12916-020-01622-w. https://bmcmedicine.biomedcentral.com/articles/10.1186/s12916-020-01622-w#citeas

27) Allin, S. et al. (2020). Comparing Policy Responses to COVID-19 among Countries in the Latin American and Caribbean (LAC) Region. https://openknowledge.worldbank.org/handle/10986/35002

28) Gray, R. (2020). Lack of solidarity hampered Europe's coronavirus response, research finds.

https://horizon-magazine.eu/article/lack-solidarity-hampered-europe-s-coronavirus-response-research-finds.html

29) Macri, J. (2016). Australia's Health System: Some Issues and Challenges. Journal of Health & Medical Economics. https://health-medical-economics.imedpub.com/australias-health-system-some-issuesand-challenges.php?aid=8344

30) Layland, A. et al. (2018). Are rankings the best way to determine healthcare systems? https://healthmanagement.org/c/healthmanage ment/issuearticle/are-rankings-the-best-way-to-determine-healthcare-systems

31) Jabukowski, E. et al. (1998). Public Health and Consumer Protection Series SACO 101 EN. Health care systems in the EU: A comparative study.
https://www.europarl.europa.eu>saco>pdf

32) Zhai, S. et al. (2017). A study on the equality and benefit of China's national health care system. International Journal for Equity in Health. https://dx.doi.org/10.1186%2Fs12939-017-0653-4.
https://www.ncbi.nlm.nih.gov/pmc/articles/PM C5575878/

33) Azevedo, M. J. (2017). The State of Health System(s) in Africa: Challenges and Opportunities. In: Historical Perspectives on the State of Health and Health Systems in Africa, Volume II. African Histories and Modernities. Palgrave Macmillan, Cham. https://doi.org/10.1007/978-3-319-32564-4_1. https://link.springer.com/chapter/10.1007/978-3-319-32564-4_1

Nijssen, E. J., Douglas, S. P., Bressers, P., & Nobel, A. (1999, July). Attitudes towards the purchase of foreign products: extending the model. In AM-AMA Global Marketing SIG Conference.

35) Christine Sperr (2017). https://www.linkedin.com/pulse/status-symbols-around-world-christine-sperr/

36) Hirsch, E. (1983). Cultural literacy. *The American Scholar*, *52*(2), 159-169. Retrieved from http://www.jstor.org/stable/41211231

37) http://www.oecd.org

38) https://www.antislavery.org/

39) Wheelen, T. L., & Hunger, J. D. (2002). Strategic Management and Business Policy, Eight Edition.

www.ingramcontent.com/pod-product-compliance
Lightning Source LLC
Chambersburg PA
CBHW050533280326
41933CB00011B/1572